The winter garden

Cover: the native *Helleborus foetidus* is one of the most useful of these lovely winter-flowering perennials
Overleaf: the bright red stems of *Cornus alba* 'Sibirica' appear even more striking against the gold and green foliage of *Elaeagnus* x *ebbingei* 'Gilt Edge' (both photographs by Michael Warren)

The winter garden

A Wisley handbook

Robert Pearson

Cassell

The Royal Horticultural Society

Cassell Educational Limited
Artillery House, Artillery Row
London SW1P 1RT
for the Royal Horticultural Society

First published 1989

British Library Cataloguing in Publication Data

Pearson, Robert
  The winter garden. — (Wisley handbooks).
  1. Gardening
  I. Title II. Series
  635 SB450.97
  ISBN 0-304-31144-8

Photographs by Michael Warren and W. H. D. Wince
Design by Lesley Stewart
Phototypesetting by Chapterhouse Ltd. Formby
Printed in Hong Kong by Wing King Tong Co. Ltd

Contents

'Lane', one of the best yellow-foliaged forms of the Lawson cypress, *Chamaecyparis lawsoniana*

Introduction

One of the most encouraging trends of recent times has been the greatly increased interest in the winter garden. One can sense a feeling in the air that this season has more to offer, much more, than had previously been realized, and its enjoyment, for weather reasons alone, is of a different kind to that experienced during the rest of the year.

With the notable exception of large plantings of highly colourful, winter-flowering heathers, especially when associated with conifers of contrasting shapes, colours and sizes, the winter garden should not be expected to provide the kind of mass spectacles so easy to arrange in most gardens of reasonable size at other seasons. The pleasures of the winter garden tend to be more individualistic, but none the less beguiling.

In winter one takes in the detail of flower, leaf and berry with enhanced perception, and thrills to the artistry of nature in countless ways. It might be the air of mystery of a group of trees and shrubs in the early morning mist, or the beautiful patterns and colourings of tree barks – some shrub barks too – when they are lit by low midday sun. It could be the set of a tree's branches, leafless and thrown into sharp relief, or the perfect form of some conifer.

An indispensable winter-flowering evergreen is the laurustinus, *Viburnum tinus*, which has been in British gardens for three centuries. Mahonia hybrids such as *Mahonia* × *media* 'Charity' and 'Lionel Fortescue', with the bonus of magnificent foliage, are other evergreens which whet the appetite. And so one could go on, and on.

Of course, we are lucky in these islands. Not only have we got, arguably, the finest climate in the world for adventurous gardening, but we are heirs to a garden flora of almost unimaginable richness. This Aladdin's cave of treasures includes much of relevance to winter, as I show in the pages which follow. Trees, shrubs, conifers, herbaceous perennial and bulbous plants are all represented here. So let us move on to the detail, allowing that in a book of this length I have had to be selective in my choice of plants. Also, I would emphasize that the plant dimensions I have given are intended as a guide only, for these can vary according to the growing conditions. So can flowering times, depending on the weather, by as much as several weeks – witness the very mild winters at the end of the 1980s.

Creating winter effects

If we all had the artistry of the best garden designers, how wonderful it would be. Of course, we haven't, but I am constantly amazed at the achievements of so many gardeners faced with garden-making challenges. Enthusiasm and a degree of imaginative insight, allied to a good working knowledge of plants, are the qualities most needed to achieve success, plus large doses of realism. The learning process for all of us never ceases.

When choosing plants for the garden and finding them homes, there is a need – even a duty – to give prime consideration to their cultural requirements. This might sound blindingly obvious, but it is remarkably easy to get so carried away that plants are put where you would most like to see them, and to just hope that all will be well. Sometimes it might be, but more often it won't.

I'm not thinking of anything as extreme as attempting to grow lime-hating plants in alkaline soils, or even subjecting plants which demand sharp drainage to soils which retain more than average amounts of moisture. It is more a question of committing such solecisms as putting plants which need shade in fully sunny positions (or vice versa), or those which are sensitive to cold winds in exposed places. Another common mistake is not allowing plants – trees, shrubs and conifers especially – room in which to develop properly. It is sometimes difficult to imagine that the small plant sitting in its container at your feet waiting to be planted may one day be a matronly-looking shrub of considerable size or a tree with its topmost branches 40 ft (12 m) off the ground.

That said, however, it is obviously advisable to have as many winter-decorative plants as possible in positions where they can be enjoyed to maximum advantage, which means, in practice, focusing attention on parts of the garden adjacent to the home. Key positions, too, must be those areas of the garden which are within line of sight from inside the house. Such vistas taking in plants of special significance can give enormous pleasure.

It was with thoughts like this in mind that I planted a couple of specimens of *Cotoneaster* 'Cornubia' at the bottom of my drive near the house, to provide rich autumnal and winter colour with their berries. In fact, although they are not left alone by the birds, these bright red berries, borne with such abundance, continue their display well into the new year. Opposite them, against the house wall facing south-east, a now-venerable specimen of the lovely *Garrya elliptica* (surely one of the finest of winter-flowering

The fast-growing *Garrya elliptica* is a magnificent evergreen shrub for a wall

shrubs) reaches to the eaves and delights in January and February with its mass of grey-green catkins. In view from the same vantage point, there is a brick wall clothed with the variegated form of the Persian ivy, *Hedera colchica* 'Dentata Variegata', and one of the best of the hollies for foliage effect, *Ilex aquifolium* 'Golden Queen'. (Don't expect me to know why this male, and therefore non-berrying holly was given the name 'Golden Queen' or why the female *I. × altaclerensis* 'Golden King' was so called; nobody seems to have the answer).

From within the house we can look out over a narrow raised terrace bed, where snowdrops reside, across a swathe of lawn to a specimen of the magnificent *Mahonia × media* 'Charity', some 12 ft (3.6 m) tall and a picture in December and January when its crown of striking foliage makes a backdrop for many terminal racemes of yellow flowers. Also within this same field of vision, the lavender-flowered *Crocus tommasinianus* carpets the ground

9

at the foot of a group of tall conifers in February and March; and, as winter draws to a close, the lovely spring snowflake, *Leucojum vernum*, in its *carpathicum* variety (with yellow-tipped petals rather than the green of the species), comes into bloom under cherries and ornamental crabs.

These are the kind of plantings to be found in many gardens up and down the country and they are illustrative of a few of the things which can be done to enhance the interest and beauty of the garden in winter.

Of course, every garden is different. We all have to take the opportunity to grow the plants which appeal to us and which are, as I've said, well suited to the existing conditions. Perhaps the perfect example of a fine and good-natured plant, able to put up with any reasonable garden situation and aspect, is the beautiful winter jasmine, *Jasminum nudiflorum*, which makes such a magnificent decoration for a wall or fence. The pyracanthas, or firethorns as they are called, are splendid evergreens for the walls of houses or outbuildings, again of any aspect. Their berries make a brilliant showing in autumn, and some carry the display into winter.

Crocus tommasinianus increases itself rapidly by division and seed

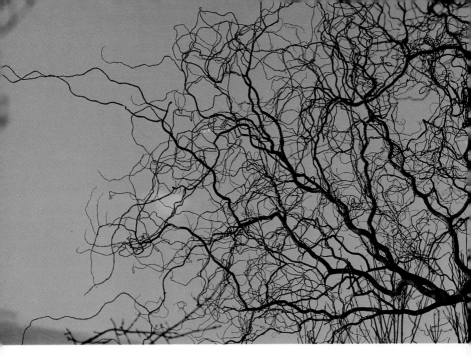

The twisted branches of *Salix matsudana* 'Tortuosa' are particularly noticeable in winter

I have already mentioned the fine evergreen foliage of the mahonias. A real tonic on any winter's day is the strong colouring of the near-indispensable *Elaeagnus pungens* 'Maculata', for its leaves cover what is a large bush with a mixture of green and golden yellow. It is always worth a prominent position.

Conifers, too, have a very special place in the winter garden for the simple reason that their shapes, colourings and foliage textures are especially prominent then. They provide a very wide range of greens, shades of yellow and blue and many different shapes from the prostrate to the bun-shaped, the cone-shaped, columnar and pyramidal. With the extremely large number of species and cultivars now available in all the leading genera, it can truly be said that there is a conifer suitable for every environment and position.

It should not be forgotten how useful a conifer screen can be to highlight the charms of winter flowers borne on bare branches, such as those of the witch hazels. The sulphur-yellow blooms of the very popular *Hamamelis* 'Pallida' have twice the impact if thrown into sharp relief in this way when lit by strong sunshine.

We are all well aware how beautiful the silhouettes of trees can be, with the tracery of bare branches and branchlets etched against a pale winter sky. Nothing quite surpasses the birches in this regard, with perhaps the elegant Swedish birch, *Betula pendula* 'Dalecarlica', my favourite. But one thinks, too, of things like the curious *Salix matsudana* 'Tortuosa', with its branches so contorted that one wonders how nature could devise such a variation from the norm; and the engaging coral bark maple, *Acer palmatum* 'Senkaki', in which the young shoots are coloured coral-red. I am sure that for most people tree silhouettes are rather low down the list of priorities when choices are being made for limited space, but I would ask you to consider this use of trees, especially when, as in the case of the birches, they have so many other virtues.

Much the same remarks apply to bark effects, which can be very beautiful. Here again the birches excel and what could be lovelier than the cherry, *Prunus serrula*, with its reddish brown, mahogany-like bark, or more exquisitely patterned than the snow gum, *Eucalyptus niphophila*? Who doesn't pause for more than a moment, too, when a bold thicket of shrubby dogwoods (*Cornus*), with their brightly coloured stems, comes into view?

For lifting the spirits sky-high, however, one has to turn to the earlier-flowering bulbs, part of whose appeal must be that winning combination of beauty and seeming vulnerability. Most, as we well know, are in physical terms quite capable of coping with our winter weather. Just think of them – the snowdrops, the winter aconites and, from February onwards, the host of crocuses, the dwarf Reticulata irises and the first of the Cyclamineus daffodils like 'February Gold'.

For obvious reasons, the number of really decorative herbaceous perennials which provide a display in winter is quite limited; but quality makes up for quantity when you recall the hellebores, especially the aristocratic-looking Corsican hellebore, *Helleborus corsicus*, as well as the delectable Algerian iris, *Iris unguicularis*, and the lovely old reddish purple-flowered *Primula* 'Wanda'.

And so we come to a pansy which, in the past few years, has taken the gardening world by storm: the F_1 Universal Strain has put an entirely different complexion on winter bedding by providing winter-long bright colour for beds and borders and for tubs, window boxes and many different kinds of container. From sowings made between May and the end of July, plants will be available for planting out in autumn, to come into flower and continue their display, in all but the worst weather conditions, until the following spring. Mixed colours are available or separate colours from purple and orange to red, shades of blue, yellow and white, some self colours, others with contrasting blotches. If you cannot raise your own plants, then garden centres offer them in

The delightful *Narcissus* 'February Gold' sometimes lives up to its name, but more often flowers in early March

the autumn, in either single or mixed colours. All in all, could you ask for more from such a splendid strain?

Perhaps our primary objective in all our garden-making (and this does not apply only to planting for winter effect) is to end up with a garden which is in harmony with itself and its surroundings. There should be no maladroit juxtaposing of plants or plant features which will strike a jarring note. One should always seek to provide interest for the eye at different levels too, which is easy enough to do using trees and shrubs with strong profiles or climbers and wall shrubs, like the ivies and the extremely handsome *Magnolia grandiflora*.

If the lawn really comes into its own between spring and autumn, that is in no way to downgrade its importance in winter. A lawn in good condition makes a marvellous foil for garden plants at all times of year, and its greenness in winter is especially to be valued.

Trees and larger conifers

TREES

A small tree which could be said to personify the spirit of the winter garden is the so-called autumn cherry, *Prunus subhirtella* 'Autumnalis', which puts on its main flush of flowering from November and continues the display in milder weather right through to late March. The semi-double white flowers, pink at the bud stage, are a delight, and for those who prefer something a little different, there is a pale pink-flowered form named 'Autumnalis Rosea'. So why should it be called the autumn cherry? It would seem that, in its native Japan, it does flower in the autumn for climatic reasons. To get the most from it in terms of winter display, it should be placed in a position protected from cold winds.

The Fuji cherry, *Prunus incisa*, makes a large bushy shrub or small tree, perhaps 15 ft tall and 18 ft wide (4.5 by 5.5 m), and opens its white flowers, which are pink at the bud stage, just as spring arrives. However, it has a form, 'Praecox', which is in bloom from late January or early February. This was raised by Hillier Nurseries of Ampfield, near Romsey, Hampshire, and so far as I am aware they are still the only suppliers.

The same nursery and many garden centres now offer the outstanding hybrid, *Prunus* 'Kursar', raised by that great authority on flowering cherries, the late Captain Collingwood Ingram (from a cross, it is thought, between *P. nipponica* var. *kurilensis* and *P. campanulata*). It is a shapely tree of upright habit which smothers itself with small pink flowers of a particularly intense colour in March, and I recall seeing it one mild winter in the full flush of its flowering in February. The leaves open a rich bronze in March, almost at the same time as the flowers, and assume orange shades in autumn.

A cherry grown not for its flowers, which have little decorative value, but for its beautiful bark effects is *Prunus serrula* from western China. This makes a tree some 20 ft (6 m) tall and rather less wide and its shining brown, peeling bark can be especially appreciated in winter. Its foliage is willow-like.

The ornamental cherries grow well in any fertile, well-drained soil, but they appreciate particularly a soil which is alkaline or near to neutral on the pH scale.

I referred earlier to the attractions of the Swedish birch, *Betula*

14

Prunus subhirtella 'Autumnalis' can grow up to 25 ft (7.6 m) high and as wide

pendula 'Dalecarlica', in its leafless winter guise. But it is grown as much or more for the beauty of the leaves, which are narrow, deeply cut and sharp-pointed, of a soft green. In 20 years or so it will become a tree some 40 ft (12 m) tall and about half that in width, but such is its light, airy appearance that it can be accommodated even in small gardens without seeming overpowering. It has the silvery trunk colouring of the species.

The cultivar of the species which is by far the best known and most widely grown is *Betula pendula* 'Youngii', or Young's weeping birch as it is called. And very lovely it is too, with its silvery bark and its domed, mushroom-like shape formed by the mass of branches and branchlets sweeping almost to the ground. It is an ideal lawn specimen or candidate for a position on a paved patio area of reasonable size, growing some 20 to 25 ft (6–7.6 m) tall in the course of time.

One of the finest of all birches for bark effect is *Betula utilis* var. *jacquemontii* from the western Himalayas, for in this case the colouring is almost startling in its whiteness. It also has good yellow autumnal leaf colouring. It will eventually make a larger tree than the Swedish birch, but graceful like all the birches.

Come to that, could anything be more graceful than the

Betula jacquemontii, as it used to be known, is now considered a variety of the Himalayan birch, *B. utilis*

common silver birch, *Betula pendula* itself, whose sobriquet "Lady of the Woods" really says it all? This can have its place too in less formal areas of the garden, ideally at the edge of a part of the garden left wild, with semi-rough grass cut only a few times a year. Then it looks in its natural element and, if three are planted close together to form an entity, so much the better. The attractive silvery bark and delicate tracery of branches give this tree enormous charm in the winter months.

But do remember that all birches are hungry trees which take a lot out of the soil. Other plants in the vicinity could feel the effects of this and may need additional feeding.

A small tree which in my experience never fails to attract attention is the coral bark maple, *Acer palmatum* 'Senkaki', which is also grown as a shrub. It takes its common name from the coral-red colouring of the younger wood. It has an erect habit of growth, as is usual with *palmatum* forms, and will take a long time to reach a height of 20 ft (6 m). It should be grown in fertile lime-free soil which is retentive of moisture in summer but still well drained, and given a sheltered position well away from any frost pocket.

I have always had a soft spot for the snake bark maples, of which *Acer pensylvanicum* from the eastern part of North America is a notable example, its bark assuming handsome white striations to contrast with the green. Its habit is erect and its eventual height about 20 ft (6 m). It is not, however, suitable for alkaline soils and, if you garden on such, then you should turn to the Asiatic kinds and particularly *A. grosseri* var. *hersii*, the bark of which is olive green striped with white. It will have a height much like that of *pensylvanicum* after a couple of decades. Both have good autumnal leaf colouring, yellow in the case of *pensylvanicum*, red and orange with *grosseri* var. *hersii*.

The evergreen strawberry trees, which bear white pitcher-shaped flowers and red strawberry-like fruits late in the year, belong to the great Ericaceae family. They are remarkable not only for their beauty but for being lime-tolerant in a plant family which, with a few exceptions, consists of lime-haters. Of the three species and one hybrid available it is the last-mentioned, *Arbutus × andrachnoides* (a cross between *A. unedo*, a native of the Mediterranean region and south-west Ireland, and *A. andrachne*, a native of south-east Europe), which is most suitable for garden planting. It is especially lime-tolerant and bears its flowers in November or early spring, with the dark green, toothed leaves providing a telling foil. The bark is coloured brownish red and is extremely attractive.

Growth is slow but, like the species, it will eventually make a

The moosewood, *Acer pensylvanicum*, was the first of the snakebark maples to be introduced to cultivation

low-branched tree. To ensure successful establishment, it is necessary to plant a young specimen straight from the pot in which it has been raised, either in spring or early autumn. The site should be sheltered from cold winds and not near a frost pocket.

Numerous willows have attractive bark colourings, among them the bright yellow-stemmed *Salix alba* var. *vitellina* and the orange-red-stemmed S. *alba* 'Britzensis' ('Chermesina'), the golden willow and the scarlet willow respectively. The first becomes a large and the second a sizable tree in the normal course of events, but they can both be stooled (hard pruned each spring) once they have grown main stems of several feet in height, and so be kept small and produce a supply of young, highly coloured wood. The colour intensity increases as the winter advances and makes for a very decorative feature.

I have never felt the urge to add the extraordinary form of the Peking willow, *Salix matsudana* 'Tortuosa', to my garden, but I can well understand its appeal, for the remarkable contortions of its branches and branchlets demand attention, particularly in winter. This cultivar from northern China has been dubbed the dragon's claw willow, and it is especially lovely when the new leaves open a fresh green colour in spring.

Willows, of course, love plenty of moisture at the roots, but they are suitable for growing in all soils which do not dry out excessively.

The snow gum, *Eucalyptus niphophila*, has proved to be remarkably hardy in Britain as eucalypts go; so, of course, has that much longer resident in our gardens and therefore far better-known species, *E. gunnii*, the cider gum. Both are extremely attractive in terms of foliage and bark colouring, particularly *E. niphophila*. Even so, they should not be expected to cope with the conditions prevailing in very cold, exposed gardens.

The snow gum in its natural habitat grows at heights of up to 6,500 ft (2,000 m) in the mountains straddling the states of New South Wales and Victoria in Australia. The patterns which form on its bark as it matures are like beautiful abstract paintings in soft shades of green, grey and cream, while the branchlets are coloured red in winter before assuming a bluish white bloom in

The scarlet willow, *Salix alba* 'Britzensis', is more of a shrub when hard pruned for winter effect

spring. The leaves are large, grey green and glossy. All in all it is a dream of a small tree which can reach a height of 20 ft (6 m) in ten years.

Eucalyptus gunnii is much faster growing and makes a tree at least 40 ft (12 m) in height, with juvenile, rounded foliage of bright silvery blue and adult foliage of lanceolate shape and a distinctive jade green. Flower arrangers like to stool their plants each spring to get a regular supply of juvenile foliage.

Eucalypts are best planted in late spring or early June, when there is no more chance of frost occurring, straight from the pots in which they have been raised. A sunny, sheltered position should be chosen where the soil is not lacking in moisture. In particular, make sure that the soil does not dry out in the months following planting. They are not suitable for growing on thin, chalky soils.

The Cornelian cherry, *Cornus mas*, is sometimes seen as a small tree, perhaps 20 to 25 ft (6–7.6 m) tall, and at other times as a large shrub. It bears clusters of yellow flowers on the bare stems in late winter and these may be followed by red, oblong fruits, from

The snow gum, *Eucalyptus niphophila*, is relatively slow-growing and hardy

Left: *Cornus mas*, a European native, has been cultivated for centuries in Britain
Right: the hybrid crab, *Malus* 'Red Sentinel', was highly rated in Dutch trials in the early 1980s

which a preserve can be made. This is an occasion when a dark background, such as might be provided by a dark green conifer screen, is a great help to throw the flowers into strong relief. Its growth is slow, which might not be a disadvantage in smaller gardens. Plant it in a sunny position in well-drained soil, which can be acid or alkaline.

The fruiting ornamental crabs, which give such a magnificent display in autumn, can in some cases continue deep into winter (mid- to late December). The popular and readily available *Malus* 'Golden Hornet', with large, egg-shaped fruits of rich yellow, is a good example, and even more so 'Red Sentinel', which can hold on to its deep red, rather round fruits until the latter part of winter. This pair make trees at least 25 ft (7.6 m) tall and wide.

My real favourites, though, are the two small-growing *Malus × robusta* forms known as 'Red Siberian' and 'Yellow Siberian', both fine trees which bear heavy crops of their cherry-like fruits, red in the first, yellow in the second, as the names suggest. The fruits hang on the trees well into winter (until some time in December in my experience), and I have a specimen of 'Yellow Siberian' quite close to my study window so it is under close observation. Both carry a profusion of white, pink-tinged flowers in spring.

Culturally, the ornamental crabs are very adaptable, doing well in any fertile, well-drained soil in sunshine or light shade, although the best fruiting will be obtained when the trees are exposed to plenty of sunshine.

21

The mountain ashes (members of the Aucuparia section of the genus *Sorbus*) include numerous species and hybrids with outstanding fruiting qualities, but many have finished their display by the time winter arrives. *Sorbus esserteauiana* is one of the exceptions, for its scarlet fruits colour up late, in October, and are usually around into the new year. It is an attractive tree with a somewhat pyramidal habit, growing eventually to some 40 ft tall and 25 ft wide (12 by 7.6 m).

Another reliable early-winter performer is *Sorbus hupehensis*, perhaps 25 ft tall and up to 20 ft wide (7.6 by 6 m). This is a very pretty tree with its purplish brown stems, bluish green leaflets and white, pink-suffused berries, which remain on the tree long after the leaves have gone, often until the turn of the year. Both *esserteauiana* and *hupehensis* put on a good show of autumn leaf colour, in shades of red. They also bear abundant white flowers in May and early June. They have no fads regarding cultivation, doing well in any average soil in sunshine or light shade.

Of the female (berrying) hollies, most people who have made a study of them would probably agree that *Ilex aquifolium* 'J. C. Van Thol' is one of the very best. Dark green, evergreen leaves, which are almost spineless and glossy-surfaced, make a fine backdrop for the mass of bright red berries. Eventually it can reach a height of 30 ft with a width of 15 ft (9 by 4.5 m), but after ten years it is likely to be still only some 10 ft (3 m) tall. Hollies are far from fast growing. 'Madame Briot' is another excellent cultivar of *I. aquifolium* for producing berries. These are an intense red, combined with heavily spined leaves which are strongly marked with deep yellow. A lot smaller than these is the attractive *I. aquifolium* 'Handsworth New Silver', with creamy white-margined leaves, long and heavily spined, which complement beautifully the red berries. The superb holly with yellow-variegated foliage, *I. aquifolium* 'Golden Queen', can also make a real contribution, both in its own right and as a male holly, whose presence is necessary to effect cross-pollination and get the female hollies to bear berries.

Hollies generally are undemanding, growing well in most soils and in less than perfect atmospheric conditions. However, the yellow-variegated kinds are best exposed to as much sunshine as possible to bring out their colouring fully.

The semi-evergreen, large-leaved *Cotoneaster* 'Cornubia' is a great asset to the early winter garden with its berry display. Although more often seen as a spreading shrub, it can be grown as a standard which, with the head of arching branches, reaches a height of 12 to 16 ft (3.6–4.8 m). There are other cotoneasters grown in standard form and semi-evergreen (they lose their leaves in hard weather) which should be considered – for instance, *C.*

Sorbus hupehensis is an excellent small tree for all seasons

Ilex aquifolium 'J.C. Van Thol' is a very free-fruiting holly and, like its relatives, ideal for a small garden

'Rothschildianus', with apricot-yellow berries and a height in the region of 16 ft (4.8 m); and the much smaller and extremely attractive, weeping C. 'Hybridus Pendulus', grown as a half-standard with a height of about 10 ft (3 m), which makes it an ideal tree for small gardens. It carries a profusion of red berries well into winter. In addition, there is the deciduous Himalayan species, C. *frigidus*, a round-headed tree up to 30 ft (9 m) tall with a crop of bright red berries.

All the cotoneasters are easily pleased in a cultural sense, growing well in any well drained, reasonably fertile soil in sunshine or light shade.

CONIFERS

And so to ornamental conifers, which have such an important role to play in the garden nowadays, and in winter particularly. People like the plantsman and conifer specialist, Adrian Bloom, are past-masters at using conifers effectively, and I am impressed by the way many Germans, Dutch and Swiss include them in their gardens with such style and panache, although sometimes, to our taste, perhaps a little excessively. In the past couple of decades or so there has been a great upsurge of interest in ornamental conifers of all complexions in this country, with much of the interest stimulated by, and many of the finest introductions coming from, Bloom's Bressingham Gardens and nursery.

Conifers are available now in tremendous variety to give pleasure at all times of year. In winter, for obvious reasons, they are particularly prominent in the garden scene, and their shapes and colourings, if they are disposed with skill, add much stimulation to the eye. The larger-growing ones therefore need to be chosen with special care, to make sure that they will integrate well with other features and are given the right kind of growing conditions.

Shapes, of course, draw the eye like a magnet, as do such colours as yellow and blue. This is in no way to underestimate green – surely the most important colour in the garden with its extraordinary range of hues, some of great subtlety. One calls to mind the dark green of the magnificent Serbian spruce, *Picea omorika*, and of the soaring, ultra-slim incense cedar, *Calocedrus* (*Libocedrus*) *decurrens*, the rich green of *Chamaecyparis lawsoniana* 'Green Pillar' and 'Kilmacurragh', and the grey green of *C. lawsoniana* 'Fletcheri', with its bronze overtones in winter.

So far as I am concerned, there is no more beautiful conifer for a key position in the garden than the Serbian spruce. It is the epitome of grace, with its thick covering of dark green leaves borne on branches which curve down only to lift up again at the tips, and this combined with a narrowly pyramidal shape. A fairly average height is 50 ft (15.2 m), with a width of some 15 ft (4.5 m) at its widest point, but it will still have reached only about 12 to 15 ft (3.6–4.5 m) in height after ten years, and it is a splendid lawn specimen. It can be grown on both acid and alkaline soils provided these are fertile and well drained. In nature it is found only in the limestone mountains which abut the River Drina in Yugoslavia.

The incense cedar has an equally striking appearance, narrowly columnar to a height of 50 ft (15.2 m) or more and with a width of 8 to 10 ft (2.4–3 m), but again slow growing – only 10 ft (3 m) after ten years. It is the ultimate in accent plants, either planted on its own or in a group of three in a lawn setting, but to do such a feature justice needs more space than most of us have at our disposal. Grow it in a sunny position in a moisture-retentive soil of good quality.

The Colorado spruce, *Picea pungens*, from the south-western United States, has provided us with a selection of cultivars of varying form, and none more calculated to catch the eye than the blue spruces of conical habit and, eventually, large size, 30 ft (9 m) or more, although they are unlikely to exceed 8 ft (2.4 m) in the first ten years. These associate delightfully with other conifers of

Left: *Chamaecyparis lawsoniana* 'Green Pillar' demonstrates how valuable green can be in the garden
Right: *Picea pungens* 'Koster' is one of the most popular blue spruces

different sizes, shapes and colourings and with heathers. They also make fine lawn specimens. They should be grown in good soil which does not lack moisture and in sheltered positions well protected from icy winds. Two of the best and most widely grown are 'Hoopsii' and 'Koster', with 'Hoopsii' having the edge for quality. Both have silvery blue colouring.

Still on the blue theme, I have been much impressed by *Chamaecyparis lawsoniana* 'Pembury Blue', which will grow to a height of about 10 ft (3 m) in as many years but can in time make a tree 40 to 50 ft (12 –15.2 m) tall. It has an attractive conical habit and blue-grey leaf sprays which tend to deepen in colour in winter. Without question, it is one of the best conifer introductions of recent times, certainly among the blues.

A very distinctive bluish green conifer is *Chamaecyparis lawsoniana* 'Wisselii', conical in habit and with unusual upward-facing, tufty growths. It grows to a height of about 40 ft (12 m), but only a quarter of that after ten years. A splendid bluish grey accent conifer, especially favoured for planting with heathers, is the slim *Juniperus scopulorum* 'Skyrocket' – up to 20 ft (6 m) tall eventually while still very narrow.

Conifers, with heathers and variegated ivy, contribute a range of colours to the winter garden

What is good among the larger yellow-foliaged conifers? Undoubtedly *Chamaecyparis lawsoniana* 'Lane', or 'Lanei' as it used to be called. This has the merit of holding its colour well in winter, and can be a dominant feature when fully grown to a height of perhaps 50 ft (15.2 m). However, it won't be more than 10 ft (3 m) tall after a decade of growth in most gardens, so there is no need to rule it out on the score of height. Few conifers are better for terminating a vista in a largish garden. Exposure to as much sunshine as possible will bring out to the full its golden yellow colouring.

An up and coming Dutch-raised cultivar of the Lawson cypress is 'Golden Wonder', with a conical habit and bright golden yellow colouring which has much in common with 'Lane' but more density. There is now another Dutch introduction in this colour band – a sport of *C. lawsoniana* 'Fletcheri' named 'Yellow Transparent', the allusion being to the pale yellow, rather translucent colouring of the young foliage, which assumes bronze tones in winter.

Still with the Lawson cypresses, 'Green Pillar' and 'Kilmacurragh' have many uses in the garden, both narrowly columnar and the second especially so. 'Green Pillar' is bright green and 'Kilmacurragh' a deeper green but just as rich. Both grow to about 10 ft (3 m) tall in a decade, with eventual heights of 35 to 40 ft (10.6–12 m). An ordinary, well-drained soil of average fertility is suitable for them.

One of the most interesting of the newer conifers is a form of the American arbor-vitae, *Thuja occidentalis* 'Smaragd' (it originated in Denmark, hence the rather unusual name). It has bright emerald-green colouring and makes a splendid hedge with its coiffured, pyramidal appearance and height, when so used, of about 7 ft (2 m) upwards. It is also an excellent specimen plant, which will in the end top the 20 ft (6 m) mark. It is an attractive feature in the winter garden and is as good for chalk soils as those of an acid nature.

(Some further suggestions may be found in the Wisley handbook, *Trees for small gardens*.)

Shrubs and climbers

SHRUBS

Shrubs are the life-blood of the modern garden – available in tremendous diversity, needing little routine attention compared with many other types of plant and always a source of potential or actual interest. They exude an air of informality which is very agreeable, whether or not they are at their season (or seasons) of greatest decorative value. Those of an evergreen nature have a special significance, of course, in winter, for they are the plants which, together with conifers, give substance to the design of the garden when deciduous trees and shrubs are leafless and so much else is taking a seasonal rest.

Nowadays, most of us tend to favour mixed borders of shrubs, perennials, bulbous plants and even annuals, although borders devoted solely to shrubs or perennials still have their place. But whichever it is, planting plans need very careful thought – as much, in the case of shrubs, about the year-round spread of interest as about the way the chosen plants will integrate with each other. In all gardens there are key vantage points and, as far as possible, one should make sure that from these there is always something to catch the eye, whatever the season. Fortunately, there is no lack of suitable material to realize such aspirations in winter.

It is a good idea also to include at least a smattering of shrubs which can be cut for indoor arrangements; these, to be enjoyed at close quarters, are especially valued in winter. There are many delightful garden shrubs which double up in this way, from the evergreen *Garrya elliptica* in all its midwinter catkinned splendour to such deciduous subjects as the winter jasmine, *Jasminum nudiflorum*, the winter sweet, *Chimonanthus praecox*, and choice viburnums like the tall *Viburnum × bodnantense* 'Dawn' and 'Deben' – the last three deliciously scented. I am no flower arranger, but I do know that I have come to appreciate, as I am sure many of you have, the true beauty of plants through the artistry of those skilled in this art form. (See also the Wisley handbook, *Flower arranging from the garden*.)

It might be thought that the grandest and most imposing of all winter shrubs are the *Mahonia × media* hybrids, which have resulted from crossing *M. japonica* and *M. lomariifolia* (both fine plants, and the latter especially beautiful but alas too tender for

Above: the early-flowering *Stachyurus praecox* is another lovely shrub
for flower arranging
Below: *Mahonia x media* hybrids like the well-known 'Charity' are
especially welcome for their showy flowers and superb foliage

many of us to grow in our gardens). These include 'Charity', the first to be introduced and widely available; 'Lionel Fortescue', which is now considered the pick of the bunch; 'Winter Sun'; 'Buckland'; 'Underway'; and 'Charity Sister'. All have superb evergreen foliage of dark green; each leaf consists of up to 21 large, spiny leaflets with, in 'Charity' for instance, the total length of the leaf exceeding 1½ ft (45 cm). All have equally superb terminal sprays of flowers, borne in November and December, in varying shades of yellow. The racemes, up to 20 in each head, may be upright or more spreading depending on the cultivar. Likewise, there are variations in size and habit. 'Charity' is upright growing and up to about 14 ft (4.2 m) tall. 'Lionel Fortescue' is more bushy and not much less in height, while 'Underway' is quite a lot shorter and very bushy, to refer to three which I have in my garden. 'Underway' is a very good plant – they all are – but it has been neglected by the nursery trade for some reason, and I know of only one source for it at the time of writing (Bridgemere Garden World, a real plantsman's garden centre, at Bridgemere, near Nantwich, Cheshire, which is able to supply personal shoppers only but has all the cultivars mentioned above).

Quite apart from their outstanding decorative qualities when in flower, these mahonias give good value throughout the year with their dramatic foliage. They grow well in any fertile, well-drained soil which is reasonably retentive of moisture in summer and does not lie wet in winter.

The viburnums, both deciduous and evergreen, provide unrivalled service to us gardeners around the year in their numerous manifestations. For winter effect alone we can call on such diverse plants as the low-growing *Viburnum davidii*, 2 to 3 ft tall and up to 5 ft wide (60–90 cm by 1.5 m), which is so much used nowadays as a ground-cover shrub; the medium-sized to large *V. farreri* (the former *V. fragrans*); the large *V. × bodnantense* 'Dawn', and its counterpart of East Anglian origin, 'Deben' (raised at Notcutt's nursery, Woodbridge); and the ever reliable and most decorative evergreen *V. tinus*, the laurustinus, a real veteran which has come up with splendid modern forms like 'Gwenllian' and 'Eve Price'.

Viburnum davidii has found its true métier as a ground-cover shrub of excellence, and the handsome, narrowly oval, evergreen leaves with their prominent veining, dark green colour and leathery texture making an attractive carpet throughout the year. If you plant some male specimens with the females, then there is always the chance of getting a good show of the turquoise-blue berries, which continue well into winter.

The deciduous *Viburnum farreri*, which eventually makes a

Viburnum x *bodnantense* 'Dawn', a vigorous, upright shrub
which produces dense clusters of flowers

bush some 10 to 12 ft (3–3.6 m) tall and wide, is very space
effective, for it bears its clusters of white, highly fragrant flowers,
pink at the bud stage, from around the beginning of November
until at least the end of February. The two *V.* × *bodnantense*
hybrids, 'Dawn' and 'Deben', both shrubs up to 10 ft tall and 4 to
5 ft wide (3 by 1.2–1.5 m), are a picture when the bare branches are
studded with the clusters of strongly fragrant flowers. In 'Dawn',
these are pink and remarkably resistant to frost damage, appear-
ing from early December to late February usually, although the
season can be some weeks longer. In 'Deben', the flowers are
white, opening from pink buds, and in milder weather they can
last from November until April.

If the flowers of the laurustinus, *Viburnum tinus*, lack scent,
they certainly make up for it in the length of the flowering period –
November to April, with only severe weather temporarily halting
the display. A popular cultivar is the compact-growing 'Eve
Price', a bush some 8 ft (2.4 m) tall which has white flowers with a
hint of pink in them opening from carmine buds. As in the other
cultivars, the dark green, oval, evergreen leaves with their glossy
surfaces are a pleasing foil. The one I like best of all, however, is
'Gwenllian', in which pale pink flowers open from pink buds and,
uncharacteristically, are often accompanied by small blue berries
– a delightful sight intermingled with the blooms. This too grows

about 8 ft (2.4 m) tall and much the same in width. There is also a new white-flowered cultivar named 'Israel', which we shall probably hear more of in future.

All these viburnums can be grown in ordinary, well-drained soils which are retentive of plenty of moisture. Positions open to sunshine are best, although *V. tinus* is tolerant of shade.

Seen at its best, the evergreen *Viburnum rhytidophyllum* is a magnificent tall foliage shrub for growing in semi-shade against a wall, where it will be protected from wind, which soon damages the leaves. These are up to 7 in. (18 cm) long, oval, dark green, shiny and wrinkled, and are carried on a plant which can reach a height of 15 to 20 ft (4.5–6 m). The yellowish white flowers, borne in trusses and opening in May and June, are a very secondary feature. The fruits which follow are at first red, then black. This needs a good-quality soil, acid or alkaline, to thrive.

The daphnes include several winter-flowering shrubs with memorable fragrance, one of the most frequently grown being, of

As well as richly coloured blossom early in the year, *Daphne mezereum* bears attractive red berries in autumn

course, the mezereon, *Daphne mezereum*. This deciduous species produces purplish red flowers in February and March, clustered thickly up the stems on a plant 3 to 4 ft (90 cm–1.2 m) tall and wide. It does well on alkaline or acid soils, and its only fault is that it is sometimes liable to die without warning, owing, it is thought, to a virus infection.

Daphne odora 'Aureo-marginata' (it is best to grow this form rather than the somewhat tender species) bears dense heads of highly fragrant, white, pink-tinged flowers, reddish purple on the outside, in late winter and early spring, these framed by handsome, lanceolate, evergreen leaves which are margined with creamy white. Find it a sheltered spot where the soil is fertile and well drained but not liable to dry out in summer. Eventually, it may reach a height of as much as 6 ft (1. 8m) but only after many years.

Still available only in restricted quantities, *Daphne bholua* 'Gurkha', which is deciduous, and 'Jacqueline Postill', which is evergreen, are wonderfully fragrant forms of this Himalayan daphne. The first was discovered by Major Spring Smythe in Nepal in 1962 at 10,000 ft (3,000 m), and the second is a seedling from it raised by Mr Alan Postill and named for his wife. 'Gurkha' carries purplish rose flowers between December and February on a bush up to 7 ft (2 m) tall, and the similarly sized 'Jacqueline Postill' has reddish mauve flowers, white on the inside, over a rather longer period into March. Both were introduced to the gardening public by Hillier and can now be obtained from a few other suppliers. Again, they require a good soil, acid or alkaline, well drained but retentive of moisture, and a position sheltered from cold wind.

The spurge laurel, *Daphne laureola*, a native of Europe, including Britain, and western Asia, is a very different proposition: a low-growing evergreen, 2 to 4 ft tall and up to 4 ft wide (60 cm–1.2 m by 1.2 m), it bears a wealth of glossy, lanceolate, leathery leaves among which nestle yellowish green flowers, scented but insignificant looking. It does well even in dense shade and is worth growing for its foliage effect. So is *Sarcococca humilis*, another evergreen for shade, which is 1½ ft tall and some 2½ ft wide (45 by 76 cm) and increases by suckers. The shiny, dark green leaves are narrowly oval and pointed, and fragrant white flowers are carried in tufty racemes in late winter. This and other sarcococcas are often known as Christmas box. Both they and the spurge laurel do well on alkaline soils.

Other shade-loving evergreens for winter effect which must not be overlooked are the skimmias, most of all perhaps in the shape of the hybrid *Skimmia × foremanii*. The mid-green leaves tend

Above: *Daphne odora* 'Aureo-marginata' starts flowering in late winter
and continues until spring
Below: the bronzy red buds of *Skimmia japonica* 'Rubella' are
decorative well before the flowers actually open

'Crotonifolia' and other forms of *Aucuba japonica* will succeed even in the shade of trees

towards the elliptic in shape and form a splendid backdrop for the mass of red berries, which last through the winter, and for the fragrant white flowers in April and May. It is a female form which needs pollinating by a male skimmia to produce berries, and what better than *S. japonica* 'Rubella'? This bears large panicles of red buds the winter through, which open to highly perfumed, white flowers in early spring. It is a slightly smaller plant than *S. × foremanii* – 3 to 4 ft (90 cm–1.2 m) tall and wide against the other's 4 to 5 ft by 6 ft (1.2–1.5 by 1.8 m). Both are suitable for alkaline soils, or any soil which is fertile and well drained, and they provide good ground cover.

In a different category, but a fine evergreen for shade, is the aucuba, *Aucuba japonica*, in its various forms. It has an affinity with the skimmias in that the sexes occur on separate plants, so that to obtain berries on the female forms a male form must be in the vicinity to effect pollination. The berries are borne in autumn and often persist long into winter. Of the female forms a good choice would be 'Crotonifolia', in which the large leaves are speckled with golden yellow and the bright red berries are freely produced. A fine male form is 'Picturata', which also has leaves marked with golden yellow. Both make bushes some 6 to 8 ft (1.8–2.4 m) tall and wide, and will do well in any average soil. The aucubas were great favourites with the Victorians and it is about time they were taken more notice of again.

Fatsia japonica and × *Fatshedera lizei* (the bigeneric hybrid which resulted from crossing *F. japonica* with the Irish ivy, *Hedera helix* 'Hibernica') are dual role home-cum-garden plants of real value. These evergreen shrubs can be extremely useful for growing in shady places, although the fatshedera will do equally well in sun, and in time, they become sizable bushes. Their handsome, shiny leaves are large, palmate and of leathery texture, up to 15 in. (38 cm) or even more across in the case of *F. japonica*, 10 in. (25 cm) in the case of × *F. lizei*. Both carry terminal panicles of flowers in October and November, although the green flowers of × *F. lizei* rarely mature out of doors. The globular umbels of white flowers of *F. japonica*, on the other hand, are a real decorative feature and are followed by black fruits. They should be grown in sheltered positions in soil of good quality.

Any deciduous shrub which produces its flowers in March, or as early as February given half a chance by the weather, and combines with that a winsome charm is worth our attention. Such a shrub is *Stachyurus praecox* (*praecox*, of course, meaning very early), and it surprises me that it has not been given greater attention by gardeners, for it does well in any average soil in sunshine

Corylus avellana 'Contorta' was originally discovered in a hedgerow in Gloucestershire in the 1860s

The lovely *Hamamelis* 'Pallida' was first raised in the Royal Horticultural Society's Garden at Wisley

or light shade. Pendant racemes of pale yellow, bell-shaped flowers, each about 3 in. (7.5 cm) long and including up to 20 blooms, are strung out along the bare branches of a bush some 8 to 9 ft tall and 5 ft wide (2.4–2.7 by 1.5 m).

That leads me on, calendar-wise, to another cheery sight in February, when the hazel or cob nut, *Corylus avellana*, bears its showy yellow male catkins. The species itself is a large bush, but its curious cultivar, 'Contorta', which always creates interest, is no more than 8 ft (2.4 m) tall and wide. The extraordinary shapes of the branches earned it the common name, earlier this century, of Harry Lauder's walking stick, and it is also called cockscrew hazel – more meaningful to those who know nothing of the famous Scottish comedian. In this form, too, the catkins are a real feature. Growth is slow, but cultivation is easy in sunshine or light shade.

The witch hazels of Chinese and Japanese origin, together with the hybrids to which they have given rise, offer rich pickings for the winter gardener, producing their flowers on the bare branches between late December and late February or early March. Neutral or acid soils are certainly best for them, but they are often grown on alkaline soils. A soil rich in humus and containing plenty of nutrients is what they really like.

The general consensus of opinion seems to be that the best of the Chinese witch hazels is *Hamamelis* 'Pallida'. I go along with that. It has soft sulphur-yellow flowers of good size with excellent fragrance and makes a bush some 8 ft (2.4 m) tall and wide. Another which has much to offer is the somewhat larger *H.* 'Brevipetala', with short-petalled flowers of deep yellow and heavily scented. A splendid *H.* × *intermedia* hybrid is 'Jelena', in which the yellow flowers have coppery red overtones.

The flowers of the witch hazels are intriguing, for the petals are strap shaped and numerous. They are also as tough as old boots, frosts not worrying them at all. Shrubs like these, blooming on the bare wood, benefit greatly from a darkish background to set off the flowers when lit by the sun. It should not be forgotten that the witch hazels have excellent autumnal colour, usually yellow but shades of red and orange in 'Jelena'.

One of the success stories of the second half of this century has been the progressive building up of a range of *Camellia* × *williamsii* hybrids (crosses between *C. saluenensis* and *C. japonica*). These have great garden value for anyone who can provide a lime-free soil and, even for those who cannot, there is always the possibility of growing a few specimens in suitably sized containers in, of course, lime-free compost. But then you must be careful not to let the roots become frozen in the arctic spells of weather we get briefly in some winters; either take the plants under cover or wrap sacking thickly round the containers.

The × *williamsii* hybrids combine hardiness with fine flower form and good evergreen foliage, the last being an attraction around the year. They also have an advantage over the huge number of *Camellia japonica* cultivars (which are also excellent garden shrubs) in that they drop their spent flowers cleanly, whereas the others hang on to them in an unsightly way, necessitating regular picking over. While spring is the main flowering season, there are some hybrids which start to bloom in winter. Everything depends on the geographical location and the micro-climate they are subjected to, with sheltered gardens in places like Cornwall being well ahead of the field. Most fall within the 6 to 10 ft (1.8–3 m) height range at maturity, but some can get much bigger in very favourable environments. The one which is exceptionally early flowering, as its name implies, is 'November Pink' (introduced at the beginning of the 1950s). Its single, rose-pink flowers have been known to open in November and certainly grace the second half of winter and spring, up to May. 'St Ewe', another with single, rose-pink flowers (of 1947 vintage) is likely to

Camellia x *williamsii* 'Debbie' flowers over a long period from late winter into May

start flowering in February, as does the lovely, New Zealand-raised 'Debbie', with peony-form, rose-pink flowers. In many gardens, too, the very popular 'Donation' (one of the first to be introduced, in 1941), with semi-double, clear pink flowers, will be in flower in March. (See also the Wisley handbook, *Camellias*.)

If you have an acid soil, there is every reason to consider growing one or two of the early-flowering (March-April) rhododendrons of modest size – say Seta or 'Tessa Roza', 4 and 5 ft (1.2 and 1.5 m) tall respectively, and with flowers, in the first case, of pale pink with deeper pink striping and, in the second, of a rosy pink hue. A group of three of one kind can be very effective. (For further information, see the Wisley handbook, *Rhododendrons*.)

Evergreen foliage shrubs of real substance include the ubiquitous and always extremely attractive *Elaeagnus pungens* 'Maculata' which, given time, makes a solid bush 10 ft (3 m) tall and wide, and two slower-growing and smaller cultivars, 'Dicksonii' and 'Frederici'. In 'Maculata', the leaves are large and heavily marked with rich yellow; in 'Dicksonii', they are margined with yellow; and in 'Frederici', the colouring is reversed, with most of the rather narrow leaves coloured cream and a dark green margin. This last is a bush half the size of 'Maculata'. They respond to good treatment and should always be given a fertile soil to grow in, avoiding thin, chalky soils.

Elaeagnus × ebbingei 'Gilt Edge' is another highly decorative foliage shrub, in which the prominent evergreen leaves are broadly margined with golden yellow. This grows quite slowly to a height and spread of 6 by 5 ft (1.8 by 1.5 m). Considerably faster growing and larger is 'Limelight', which has a central blotch of yellow on its leaves. Both have leaves silvery on the undersides and can be used to good effect in the winter garden.

There are numerous easily grown cotoneasters which carry their display of red berries well into winter. Indeed, the deciduous or semi-evergreen Cotoneaster simonsii, 8 to 10 ft (2.4–3 m) tall and wide, will often keep its berries right through the winter. The same applies to the deciduous C. horizontalis, which is low growing in the open, higher against a wall, and also has prettily coloured leaves in early winter, turning red and orange and slow to fall; and to the ground-covering evergreen C. conspicuus 'Decorus', 2 to 3 ft (60–90 cm) tall by 6 ft (1.8 m) wide.

The mainstream forsythias might just, in calendar terms, squeeze into late winter to start their flamboyant flowering season, but such fine cultivars as Forsythia × intermedia 'Lynwood', 'Spring Glory' and 'Beatrix Farrand' are spring shrubs and I shall turn to a real winter flowerer, the Korean F. ovata, and its cultivar 'Tetragold'. The species makes a bush

A shapely bush of the invaluable Elaeagnus pungens 'Maculata'

some 5 ft (1.5 m) tall and wide, with arching branches bearing bright yellow flowers from late February or very early March. 'Tetragold' is a smaller version raised in Holland, with deep yellow flowers and a height and spread of about 4 ft (1.2 m). It hardly needs saying that the forsythias generally are among the easiest of deciduous shrubs to please: almost any garden soil suffices and they do well in sunshine or light shade.

No sight is more heartening on a bright winter day than the massed stems of shrubby dogwoods lit by strong sunshine and viewed perhaps across a lawn or, even better, beside some informal water feature. But they are pleasurable in many different situations. The pick of the bunch might well be *Cornus alba* 'Sibirica', with bright red, young stems, and *C. stolonifera* 'Flaviramea', in which the stems are an attractive greenish yellow. They are delightful grown together.

Hard pruning annually in spring just as growth is starting ensures a supply of young, highly coloured wood, and keeps plants to a height of about 6 ft (1.8 m). They revel in damp soil, but in fact do well in any soil of reasonable quality. Always find them a home open to plenty of sunshine.

The white-stemmed ornamental bramble, *Rubus cockburnianus*, a relative of the blackberry, is also very showy in winter. It is the first-year stems which have the attractive white bloom overlaying the purple, and the older stems should be pruned away either in autumn or early spring. It makes an open bush some 8 ft (2.4 m) tall and rather less wide, with deciduous fern-like foliage. The purplish flowers appear in early summer but are of little consequence. It is easily grown in poor soils.

Why do not more gardeners grow *Kerria japonica*, rather than its stiffer and more upright-growing, orange-yellow, double-flowered form, 'Pleniflora'? The species itself makes a lower, spreading bush 4 to 6 ft (1.2–1.8 m) tall and wide, with single, bright yellow flowers in late spring, and its vivid green stems are a joy when bare in winter. Again, it presents no problems culturally.

WALL SHRUBS AND CLIMBERS

Good use should be made of house and other tall walls to grow one or more of those evergreen pyracanthas which carry their berries over into the winter season – the excellent orange-red-berried 'Mohave', for instance, which has the additional advantage of being resistant to fireblight and scab, two diseases to which pyracanthas are prone; orange-red-berried 'Orange Glow'; and the well-known, red-berried 'Watereri', which is an excellent, free-standing specimen plant, usually some 8 ft tall and 10 ft wide

Above: frosty weather gives an extra dimension to the red stems of
Cornus alba 'Sibirica'
Below: a mixture of *Garrya elliptica* and pyracantha makes an eye-catching winter feature on a wall

(2.4 by 3 m). Another with long-persisting berries is the red-berried *Pyracantha atalantioides*, but it is probably best to steer clear of this as it is said to be susceptible to fireblight.

Similarly, a home should be found if possible for the evergreen *Garrya elliptica*, an almost indispensable component of the mid-winter garden, for there is nothing quite to compare with a full-sized specimen, possibly as much as 20 ft (6 m) tall, smothered in a grey-green waterfall of catkins during January and February. On male plants, the catkins can be as much as 12 in. (30 cm) long and certainly 9 in. (23 cm) in normal circumstances. Those of the cultivar 'James Roof' can be several inches longer still, but the species itself is rewarding enough. The smallish oval leaves are dark green and thickly borne, remaining attractive around the year. This shrub can be grown on a wall with any aspect, but do not plant it where it will be exposed to cold winds, which in extreme cases can badly brown the leaves. Provide it with a good soil. It can be grown as a free-standing shrub in many gardens, but is usually far better in a wall bed.

An evergreen wall shrub of very different mien is *Euonymus fortunei* 'Silver Queen', which doubles as an effective ground-cover shrub. Planted against a wall, it will eventually reach a height of some 10 ft (3 m). It has small oval leaves of fresh green and creamy white, taking on a pinkish tinge in winter which is

Euonymus fortunei 'Silver Queen', a small, compact shrub, grows taller against a wall

The evergreen *Clematis cirrhosa* var. *balearica* flowers from September to March

especially welcome. This is one of a range of cultivars of *E. fortunei* which have carved out a niche for themselves as highly decorative ground-cover shrubs. Others include 'Emerald Gaiety', in which the leaves are margined with silvery white and often flecked with pink in the winter months. It forms a mound some 2 ft tall and 2½ ft wide (60 by 76 cm). The very popular 'Emerald 'n' Gold', with rich golden yellow variegation and pink suffusions in winter is slightly smaller, while the even smaller 'Sunspot', which is rapidly coming to the fore, has dark green leaves enlivened by splashes of golden yellow. All grow well in any well drained soil of average quality, in sunshine or light shade.

The winter jasmine, *Jasminum nudiflorum*, is well known and very valuable for its bright yellow flowers in midwinter. The secret of keeping it in order is to prune it immediately after flowering has finished. If you don't, it can get in a real tangle. First you must form a framework of leading shoots, which are tied in to a trellis or some other support. Once that is established, then you annually, after flowering, reduce the laterals arising from these shoots to buds near the base. This brings order out of what can otherwise be chaos.

A winter-flowering climber for more favoured gardens is the fern-leaved clematis, *C. cirrhosa* var. *balearica*, which has prettily divided leaves, as the common name suggests, assuming a bronzy purple in winter. The creamy coloured bell flowers, spotted reddish purple within and less decorative than the foliage, are

45

With its neat habit of growth, *Hedera helix* 'Goldheart' is one of the finest variegated ivies

borne off and on throughout the winter. It can reach a height of 15 ft (4.5 m) or so and must be given a sheltered, sunny position.

And this brings me to the ivies, those indispensable climbers for year-round effect. Two of the most valuable must be the cultivars of *Hedera colchica*, 'Dentata Variegata' and 'Sulphur Heart' (or 'Paddy's Pride' as it used to be known). I have been amazed over the years just how much punishment both can take from the weather without any visible sign of distress. Once they get going, they can cover a vast expanse of wall space. 'Dentata Variegata' has very large, oval leaves which are an amalgam of palish green, grey green and creamy yellow; 'Sulphur Heart', with very slightly smaller, heart-shaped leaves, is a mixture of light and deeper green with bold areas of yellow. What would we do without them? In winter especially they are a real tonic.

Then, of course, there are the forms of the common ivy, *Hedera helix*. Some of the best for garden use are 'Goldheart', having dark green leaves with a central splash of bright yellow; 'Buttercup', bright yellow in full sun, with the green element increasing progressively if subjected to shade; and 'Ivalace', one of my favourites, with a very pretty five-lobed leaf of dark green and suitable for clothing a low wall, which is how I grow it.

(For some further suggestions, see the Wisley handbooks, *Shrubs for small gardens* and *Climbing and wall plants*.)

Heaths and smaller conifers

HEATHS

All those name changes! The name *Erica carnea* for the winter heath has lost place to *E. herbacea*, but now there seems at least a chance that botanists will reinstate the former name – not that it was ever superseded as far as most nurserymen are concerned. You will find both names in plant catalogues.

One thing which remains constant is the great value of the cultivars of this species, for they bring bright colour to the garden from December onwards, with most putting on their display from January. Unusually for ericaceous plants, they are lime-tolerant, and so too are the forms of the hybrid *Erica* × *darleyensis* and *E. erigena* (*E. mediterranea*).

But lime-tolerance means just that, and it is all a matter of degree. None of the above can be expected to cope with thin, chalky soils. All soils, for that matter, are best improved in texture and moisture-holding capacity (very important to heaths and heathers in dry summer periods) by digging in plenty of peat before planting, or working it into the soil when actually planting. Sunny positions are best to ensure the maximum amount of flower production, but light shade is alright if that is all that can be offered.

First, the cultivars of *Erica herbacea*, which all fall within the height range of 6 to 10 in. (15–25 cm). A superb ground cover and lovely plant with its white, brown-anthered flowers and fresh green foliage is 'Springwood White', which has a bright pink counterpart in 'Springwood Pink', perhaps less strong growing but another first-class ground cover. Both flower from January to March. 'Myretoun Ruby', with rich ruby-red flowers from February to April and dark green foliage, is one of the finest of the more recently introduced cultivars; and another of real excellence is 'Pink Spangles', which includes in its flowers glowing shades of this colour, produced from January to March. For foliage effect there is the yellow-leaved 'Foxhollow', with pink and reddish suffusions in winter (the pale lavender-pink flowers of late winter do not amount to much); and 'Vivellii', with its dark bronze foliage in winter, dark green in summer, and deep carmine-red flowers in February and March. The earliest colour comes from 'King George', which can produce its crimson-pink flowers in November, and the purplish pink-flowered 'December

The winter heaths create a carpet of colour, set off by bronze rhododendron foliage

Red'. There are numerous other cultivars to choose from.

The *Erica × darleyensis* hybrids include delightful offerings, most taller than the *E. herbacea* forms. The splendid 'Arthur Johnson', for instance, is 2 to 2½ ft (60–76 cm) tall, and flowers from November or December until early spring. Its flowers are a rich rose pink and borne most freely. Almost as long flowering is the pink 'Darley Dale' and its white-flowered sport, 'Silberschmelze', 1½ ft (45 cm) and 1¼ ft (38 cm) tall respectively. The yellow-foliaged 'Jack H. Brummage' is another shorter variety with pale pink flowers in February and March.

The *Erica erigena* cultivars are essentially spring flowering, but there is one, 'Irish Dusk', with pale grey leaves, which bears its clear pink flowers from early winter into spring.

CONIFERS

Heather plantings, being all on much the same plane, need contrasts in height, shape, colour and texture to give them maximum impact. This is easily provided by conifers, and a few of the right dimensions for the situation will make an enormous difference. Which you use depends entirely on the scale of the planting. There can be times when the tall blue spruces mentioned earlier (p.25) and the pencil-slim *Juniperus scopulorum* 'Skyrocket' (p.26) are just what is required. Another favourite for associating with heathers is *Thuja occidentalis* 'Rhiengold', with its conical habit and yellow foliage which turns a bronzy gold in winter. Although it may eventually reach a height of 10 ft (3 m), it is likely to be considerably less and in any case takes a long time to get there. Extremely attractive too and growing to only about 2½ ft (76 cm) tall after ten years is *Thuja orientalis* 'Aurea Nana'. It makes a globular bush with bright golden green, vertical leaf sprays in summer, which take on bronzy green tones in winter.

Like the larger conifers, the dwarf and slow-growing ones have much to recommend them for the winter garden, with or without heathers. Ground-hugging junipers such as *Juniperus horizontalis* 'Glauca', with thin, trailing, steely blue branches covering an area of up to 6 ft (1.8 m), are always pleasing, as is *J. squamata* 'Blue Star', which provides a quite different effect as a steely blue bush some 15 in. tall and 18 in. wide (38 by 45 cm).

Quite outstanding for providing a low mound of bright yellow is the recently introduced *Juniperus × media* 'Gold Sovereign', which holds its colour through the winter. It grows about 1½ ft tall and 2½ ft wide (45 by 76 cm) after ten years. Another cultivar, 'Old Gold', also keeps its colour around the year extremely well, and is roughly twice the size of the last.

The bronzy gold colouring of *Thuja occidentalis* 'Rheingold' is a wonderful foil for other plants in winter
Opposite: *Juniperus scopulorum* 'Skyrocket' provides a striking contrast to heathers

I have a great liking for the cultivars of the mountain pine, *Pinus mugo*, with their tufty growths. One of the best of these is 'Gnom', which is still likely to be no more than $2\frac{1}{2}$ ft (76 cm) tall and wide after a decade of growth, but can eventually reach a height and spread of 6 ft (1.8 m).

(For further information, see also the Wisley handbooks *Heaths and heathers* and *Dwarf and slow-growing conifers*.)

Perennials of consequence

Of the limited number of perennial plants which put on their display at this time of year, it is the hellebores which make by far the largest contribution. And what a contribution when one considers evergreen species and hybrids as diverse as the Corsican hellebore, *Helleborus corsicus*; the Christmas and Lenten roses, *H. niger* and *H. orientalis*; and the species which is so maligned by its name, *H. foetidus*, the so-called stinking hellebore, which only gives off an odour if its stems are crushed.

It always surprises me that the magnificent *Helleborus corsicus* does so well in this country, for it is, after all, a native of Corsica, Sardinia and the Balearic Islands, which have a very different climate. One of the best specimens I have ever seen was performing in Mull, western Scotland, admittedly in a snug, sheltered spot – as it needed to be on that windy island. It is indeed a sight to behold when in flower in March and April, the bold, tripartite leaves of greyish green surmounted by heads of pendant, bell-shaped, pale green flowers. Sometimes, too, it can be in flower in February. Like others of its kind, it prefers to grow in light shade in soil of good quality.

The Christmas rose, in flower from December to March, is a plant for a sheltered wall bed, although without the protection of a tall cloche, the attractive white blooms, with their prominent golden yellow stamens, are still likely to get badly damaged by weather and spoilt – a real consideration if they are wanted, as they so often are, for cutting for arrangement.

Helleborus orientalis is the group name for a number of hybrids which bear saucer-shaped flowers in a delightful range of colours from purplish plum to shades of maroon and pink and white with handsome petal markings of crimson or maroon. These plants, 1½ ft (45 cm) tall or perhaps a little more, provide a succession of blooms from February until early April and are especially useful for bringing to life shrub borders which are lack-lustre at that time of year.

It is usually March before the highly distinctive *Helleborus foetidus* comes into bloom with its pale green, suffused maroon flowers complemented handsomely by very dark green, almost black leaves, much divided into narrowly lanceolate segments. But flowering can start in February and it is an outstanding plant for shady positions.

Another plant of real importance is the beautiful Algerian *Iris*

Above: the wide-open flowers, spotted within, are typical of the Lenten roses

Below: *Helleborus corsicus* (left) does not bloom until its second year but is well worth waiting for; *Iris unguicularis* (right) seems to flower best in poor, dry soil where it is left undisturbed

A border in the famous winter garden at the University of Cambridge Botanic Garden, with cornuses and *Helleborus foetidus*

unguicularis, of which there are quite a lot of forms in commerce, if only from single or very few sources in each case. Two of the best are the pale blue 'Walter Butt' and purple 'Mary Barnard', but it is usually early spring before they are in flower. The species itself flowers between October and March whenever the weather is reasonably mild, and really nothing could give more satisfaction than its lilac-mauve flowers, with their lovely yellow and white markings on the lower part of the petals, rising above the mass of grassy-looking foliage. The flower colouring can be variable, from the typical palish blue shades to purple. All are very attractive. The blooms last only a few days when cut, but even so are delightful in the home.

The pulmonarias or lungworts seem to have made a comeback in recent years, and very welcome that is too for they are excellent early-flowering perennials for shade. They also provide good ground cover with their large leaves and most are evergreen. In particular, I would draw attention to *Pulmonaria rubra* 'Redstart', which can be opening its rosy red flowers in early February, to continue in bloom until May or even June. The flowers have an admirable foil in the pale green leaves. *Pulmonaria saccharata* has dark green leaves heavily spotted with silver or grey, and a delightful form of it with pink and blue flowers is named 'Margery Fish'. These pulmonarias grow well in any soil which does not lack moisture.

The bergenias are among the best of perennials for ground cover, their mass of often very handsome, evergreen foliage providing effective weed barriers, quite apart from the spring display of showy blooms. Moreover, they flourish in any well drained soil of reasonable quality, in sunshine or light shade. Their interest in the present context is that some have foliage which colours up most attractively in winter. For instance, the leaves of 'Ballawley', one of the finest of the hybrids, turn a liver-red colour; 'Abenglut' becomes maroon with the reverse of the leaves plum-red; *B. cordifolia* 'Purpurea' is purplish; and *B. purpurascens* is reddish purple.

And don't forget the pretty little *Primula* 'Wanda', which often makes a brave show in late winter with its reddish purple flowers, in light shade or sunny positions.

Bulbs

Poise, perfection of form, classical beauty – one could heap the superlatives on snowdrops, those most welcome of all winter flowers. It is always a great moment when one goes out into the garden in mid-January or thereabouts and finds such forms of the common snowdrop, *Galanthus nivalis*, as 'Viridapicis' (with green tips to the outer segments of the flower as well as the inner ones) and the hybrid *G.* 'Atkinsii' in full bloom. Then, a little later, in February, the larger *G. elwesii* puts on its show. Of course, there are many other snowdrops, but these are what I would call in the mainstream of garden cultivation.

Snowdrops like shade and soil with a good moisture content. These easy plants can sometimes be quite tricky to establish from dry bulbs in autumn, but, increasingly, "green" plants are becoming available from bulb suppliers for planting in the spring.

Another bulbous plant which I would hate to be without in my garden is *Crocus tommasinianus*, a delightful little species which establishes itself readily in light shade or sunshine and soon carpets the ground in February with its lilac-mauve flowers. Forms like 'Whitewell Purple', reddish purple, and 'Ruby Giant', purple, are often in flower quite early in the month, and are less invasive than the species.

February-March flowering, too, are the *Crocus chrysanthus* forms such as the delectable white 'Snow Bunting'; 'E. A. Bowles', pale yellow with bronze basal markings; and 'Cream Beauty' and 'Blue Pearl', which have prominent orange-red and orange stigmata respectively to add greatly to their effectiveness. They are followed in flower in March by the Dutch hybrids, which make taller plants with larger flowers. Plant these in sunny positions near the front of a mixed border, around deciduous shrubs and indeed anywhere that they will prosper (they need shelter from cold winds) and give maximum visual enjoyment. Plant the corms 3 in. (7.5 cm) deep.

Wonderfully cheery, especially when it has the temerity to poke its buttercup-like, bright yellow flowers through snow in February, is the winter aconite, *Eranthis hyemalis*. The bright green leaves form a ruff around the flowers, and it naturalizes freely under trees or around shrubs. Plant the tubers 2 in. (5 cm) deep in late summer or early autumn, as soon as you can get hold of them, for like the snowdrops they don't like being out of the ground for long.

Above: *Galanthus* 'Atkinsii' is somewhat taller than the common snowdrop
Below: *Crocus chrysanthus* forms such as 'Cream Beauty' are among the earliest crocuses to flower

Above: the winter aconite, *Eranthis hyemalis*, may appear as early as January in mild weather
Below: *Iris histrioides* 'Major' has large weather-resistant flowers, lasting for several weeks

The precocious-flowering little forms of *Iris reticulata*, some 6 in. (15 cm) tall, have exquisitely moulded flowers in lovely shades of blue, violet and purple. They need a sunny, well-sheltered home where the soil is particularly well drained and preferably alkaline. They are ideal for planting in raised beds and troughs and, of course, for pockets in the rock garden. 'Cantab', a cultivar with soft blue colouring enhanced by orange markings on the falls (outer segments), is probably the best known. Slightly shorter and coming into flower rather earlier is the excellent Reticulata iris, *I. histrioides* 'Major'. It is also somewhat more robust, and a sight to savour with its dark blue flowers with white markings on the falls. Plant the bulbs 2 to 3 in. (5–7 cm) deep in September or as soon as possible in autumn.

A hardy cyclamen which comes within our purview is the charming little *Cyclamen coum*, a mere 3 in. (7.5 cm) tall and with miniature blooms typical of the genus borne above rounded, dark green leaves, which may have silver markings. The flower colour is variable – anything from shades of red to pink and white – and it blooms between the turn of the year and late February. It is best given a lightly shaded position, humus-rich soil and especially good drainage. Plant the tubers about 1 in. (2.5 cm) deep in early autumn, but better still, if you can, find a nursery which offers pot-grown specimens for sale. Start with these for preference, for tubers offered dry can be difficult to establish if out of the ground for some time.

The pretty pale blue squill, *Scilla tubergeniana*, with stylish darker blue banding down each segment of the flower, leads its clan into bloom by a margin of some weeks. It opens its flowers in February and early March, and is followed by the fine deep blue form of the Siberian squill, *S. sibirica*, known as 'Spring Beauty', which with a height of about 8 in. (20 cm) is twice the size of *tubergeniana*. Both kinds increase freely. The bulbs should be planted 3 in. (7.5 cm) deep in autumn and be left alone to increase until they have become overcrowded, when they can be lifted, divided and replanted in late summer.

There are forms of the handsome *Anemone blanda* which come into flower in February and March – for instance, 'White Splendour', the pink 'Charmer' and 'Violet Star'. All are about 4 in. (10 cm) tall. They associate very well with deciduous shrubs, which in the summer can provide some shade from the sun. Plant the tubers 2 in. (5 cm) deep in early autumn.

What else? Well, certainly the spring snowflake, *Leucojum vernum*, the bulbous plant which looks like an oversized snowdrop. And very fine it is, with its bold, strap-shaped leaves of dark green complementing perfectly the shapely white flowers with

their green markings on the tips of the segments. I like even better the east European variety of this European native – *carpathicum*, in which the segment markings are yellow rather than green. In mild winters, both are in flower by late February or early March (even early January in 1989), so fitting comfortably into this winter survey.

One can include also some of the earliest of the *Narcissus cyclamineus* hybrids, those spendidly garden-worthy derivatives of this species crossed with trumpet daffodils. The exquisite *N. cyclamineus* itself bears its bright yellow, cyclamen-like flowers in February and March, but needs a moist soil to succeed. What beauty there is in the long trumpet and swept-back segments of its flowers. Of the hybrids, 'February Gold', as the name implies, is very early coming into bloom, although it is more likely to be the beginning of March than February. 'Peeping Tom', some 14 to 15 in. (35–38 cm) tall as opposed to the 12 in. (30 cm) of 'February Gold', also flowers in early March. Another lovely early form is the deep yellow 'Tête-à-Tête', a mere 6 in. (15 cm) tall and carrying several blooms on each stem. Everything depends on the weather and the severity of the winter as to just when these and other Cyclamineus hybrids start their display. They are marvellous for growing below deciduous shrubs, and can transform areas which would otherwise be just a mess of bare stems at that time. Plant the bulbs 3 to 4 in. (7.5–10 cm) deep in September or as soon as possible thereafter.

(For some further suggestions, see the Wisley handbook, *Growing dwarf bulbs*.)

POSTSCRIPT

Hopefully, there is enough in this to whet the appetite and indicate some of the pleasures which the winter garden is capable of providing. One of the most agreeable aspects of the British climate is its clearly defined seasonal differences – differences which provide our gardens with major sources of interest. Winter, no less than spring, summer and autumn, has much to offer.

Opposite: the variable *Cyclamen coum* usually begins flowering in January

Above: the Cornelian cherry, *Cornus mas*, with its yellow flowers
borne on slender, leafless branches, conveys the quiet charm of the
winter garden
Below: *Erica herbacea* 'King George', often wrongly called 'Winter
Beauty', continues flowering until February

Gardens to visit

The following is a selection of gardens which are notable for winter effect. All are open during the winter months but it is advisable to check times.

Barnsley House Garden, Barnsley, nr Cirencester, Gloucs

Bedgebury National Pinetum, nr Goudhurst, Kent

Beth Chatto Gardens, Elmstead Market, Essex

Glasgow Botanic Gardens, Glasgow

Harlow Car Gardens (Northern Horticultural Society), Harrogate, N. Yorks

Hillier Gardens and Arboretum, Ampfield, nr Romsey, Hants

Inverewe (National Trust for Scotland), Poolewe, Ross & Cromarty, Highland

Marwood Hill, nr Barnstaple, Devon

Mount Edgcumbe, nr Plymouth, Cornwall

Ness Gardens (University of Liverpool), Wirral, Cheshire

The Old Rectory, Burghfield, Berks

Royal Botanic Garden, Edinburgh

Royal Botanic Garden, Kew, Surrey

Royal Horticultural Society's Garden, Wisley, nr Woking, Surrey

Savill and Valley Gardens, Windsor Great Park, Berks

Threave Gardens (National Trust for Scotland), nr Castle Douglas, Dumfries & Galloway

University of Cambridge Botanic Garden, Cambridge

University of Oxford Botanic Gardens, Oxford

Wakehurst Place Garden (National Trust/RBG Kew), nr Ardingly, W. Sussex

Winkworth Arboretum (National Trust), nr Godalming, Surrey

The Winter Garden (Norfolk College of Agriculture and Horticulture), Burlingham, nr Norwich, Norfolk

Index of plants